COLIN INGRAM
DONOVAN MANNATO

HELLO ENTERTAINMENT/DAVID GARFINKLE
MJE PRODUCTIONS
ADAM SILBERMAN

PATRICIA LAMBRECHT

in association with

COPPEL/WATT/WITHERS/BEWICK FIN GRAY/MICHAEL MELNICK MAYERSON/GOULD HAUSER/TYSOE
RICHARD CHAIFETZ & JILL CHAIFETZ JEFFREY B. HECKTMAN LAND LINE PRODUCTIONS
MARION/GILBERT/SHAHAR FRESH GLORY PRODUCTIONS/BR

by special arrangement with **PARAMOUNT**

present

Book & Lyrics
BRUCE JOEL RUBIN

Music & Lyrics
DAVE STEWART & GLEN BALLARD

Based on the Paramount Pictures film written by Bruce Joel Rubin

"Unchained Melody" written by Hy Zaret and Alex North
Courtesy of Frank Music Corp. (ASCAP)

General Management
BESPOKE THEATRICALS

Production Management
AURORA PRODUCTIONS

Advertising & Marketing
SPOTCO

Press Agent
THE HARTMAN GROUP

Casting Director (US)
TARA RUBIN CASTING

Casting Director (UK)
DAVID GRINDROD

Musical Director
DAVID HOLCENBERG

Associate Director
THOMAS CARUSO

Production Stage Manager
IRA MONT

Additional Movement Sequences **LIAM STEEL**

Musical Supervisor, Arranger & Orchestrator
CHRISTOPHER NIGHTINGALE

Video & Projection Designer
JON DRISCOLL

Lighting
HUGH VANSTONE

Illusions
PAUL KIEVE

Sound
BOBBY AITKEN

Designer
ROB HOWELL

Choreographer
ASHLEY WALLEN

Director
MATTHEW WARCHUS

ISBN 978-1-4584-2327-6

7777 W. BLUEMOUND RD. P.O. BOX 13819 MILWAUKEE, WI 53213

Visit Hal Leonard Online at
www.halleonard.com

HERE RIGHT NOW

Words and Music by GLEN BALLARD,
DAVID ALLAN STEWART and BRUCE JOEL RUBIN

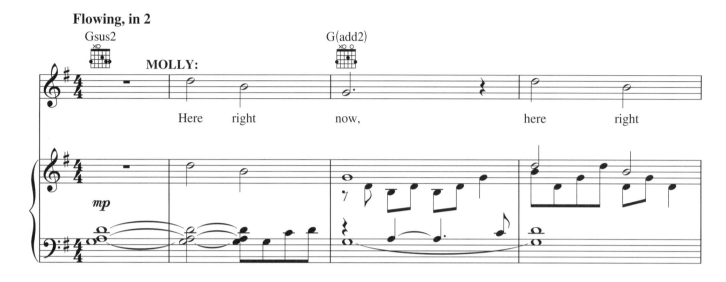

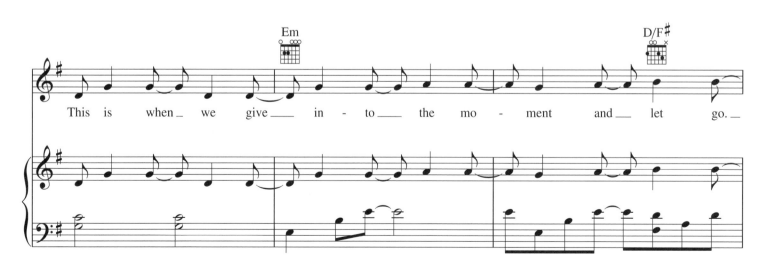

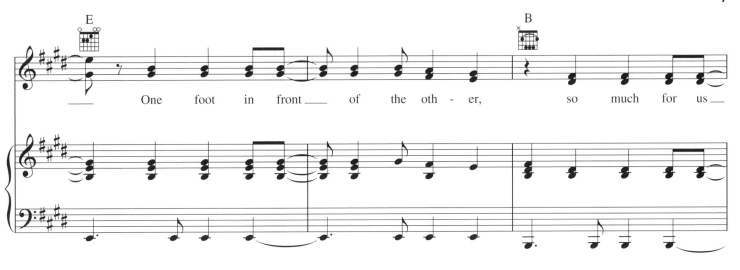

One foot in front ___ of the oth - er, so much for us ___

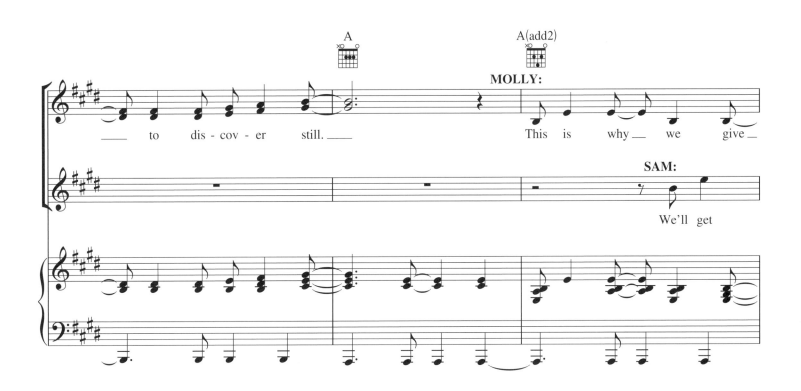

___ to dis - cov - er still. ___

MOLLY:
This is why ___ we give ___

SAM:
We'll get

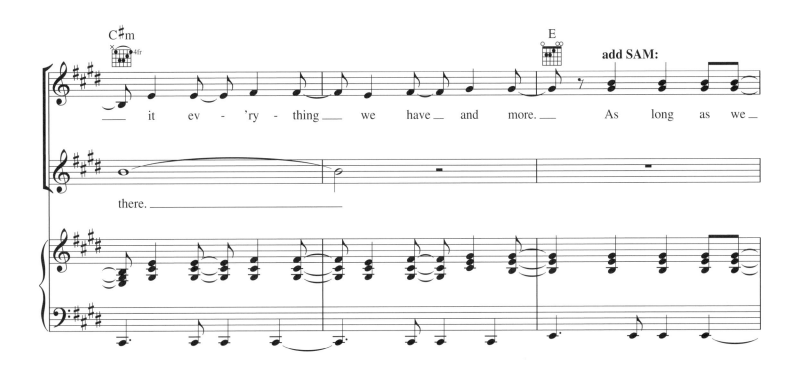

___ it ev - 'ry - thing ___ we have ___ and more. ___ As long as we ___

add SAM:

there. ___

in luck, ___ I don't be-lieve ___ in fate, ___

but this ___ is so ____ much more ___ than I _____ could e - ver con -

- tem - plate. ___ I can't ___ be-lieve ___ you walked in - to ___

___ my life ___ and you're _____ still here. ___ When I'm ___ with you ___

Add MOLLY:

UNCHAINED MELODY

Lyric by HY ZARET
Music by ALEX NORTH

MORE

Words and Music by GLEN BALLARD,
DAVID ALLAN STEWART and BRUCE JOEL RUBIN

Hurried Rock

ENSEMBLE:
More and more __ and more __ and more __ and more.

More and more __ and more __ and more __ and more. __

More and more __ and more __ and more __ and more. __

and more __ and more. __

CARL: We're just play-ing a

ENSEMBLE:

More and more __ and more __ and more __ and... Now!

num - bers __ game, and ev-'ry sec-ond the num - bers __ change.

More!

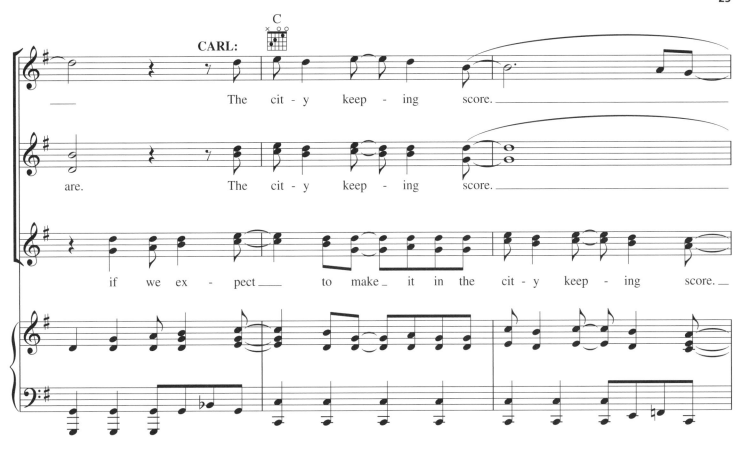

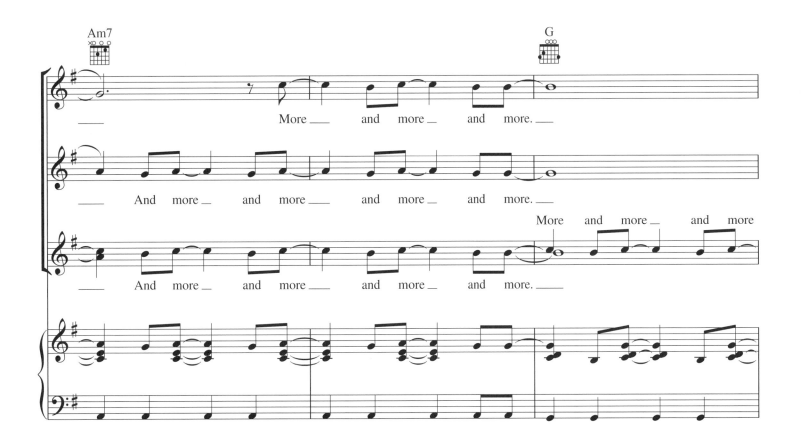

THREE LITTLE WORDS

Words and Music by GLEN BALLARD,
DAVID ALLAN STEWART and BRUCE JOEL RUBIN

SAM: I say it with my eyes, when I hold you close at night, when I make you scram-bled eggs, when I tell you silly jokes, when I say you're al - ways right.

you be-gin to fear __ it is-n't true. I'd love to hear __ it ev-'ry day, But

e - ven just this one time, it's o - kay. I can live that way. It's

not like I ev - er doubt __ it, but I'd real-ly like to hear a - bout __ it, _____ what you're

SAM:

Not like you have to doubt __ it. I don't want to have to shout __

YOU GOTTA LET GO NOW

Words and Music by GLEN BALLARD,
DAVID ALLAN STEWART and BRUCE JOEL RUBIN

HOSPITAL GHOST:

Lis-ten, young man, there's so much to tell. Let me as-sure you that this is-n't Hell. But it ain't Heav-en ei-ther, it's some-where in-be-tween. But you can't op-er-ate like you did as of late. Look a-round and you'll see what I mean.

ARE YOU A BELIEVER?

Words and Music by GLEN BALLARD,
DAVID ALLAN STEWART and BRUCE JOEL RUBIN

you can shout! You got-ta cast out your doubts. _

shout! You got-ta cast out your doubts. _

Double-time Gospel

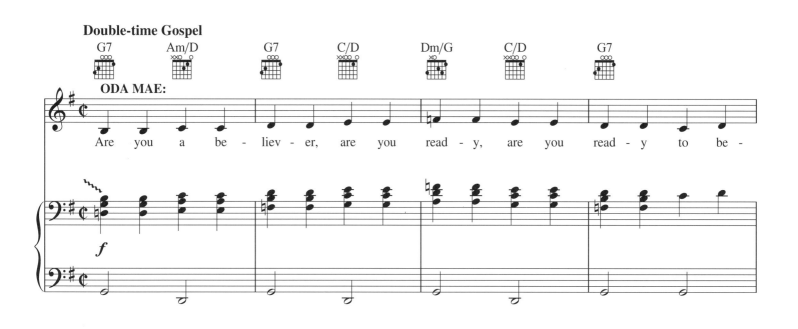

ODA MAE:

Are you a be - liev - er, are you read - y, are you read - y to be -

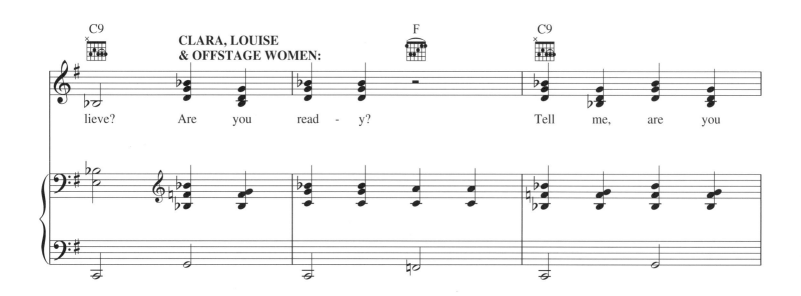

CLARA, LOUISE & OFFSTAGE WOMEN:

lieve? Are you read - y? Tell me, are you

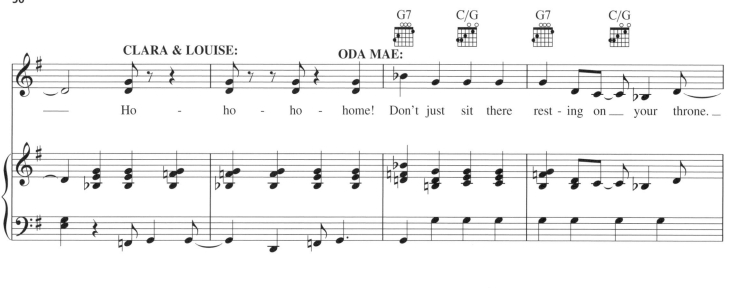

I can feel it, I know it's real. ____

I can feel it, I know it's *real. ____

Tempo I

Gm

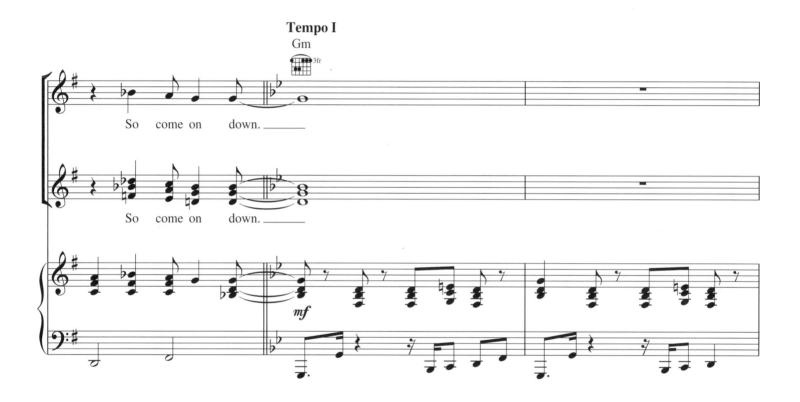

So come on down. ____

So come on down. ____

ODA MAE:

Mis-sus San-ti-a - go, it's

* *Lower two voices slide to their respective pitches.*

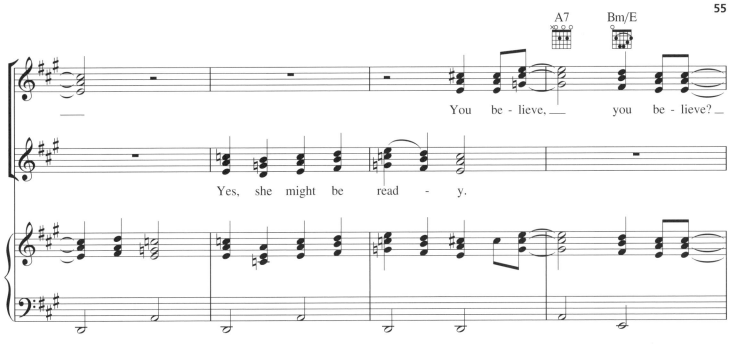

You be - lieve, _____ you be - lieve? _____

Yes, she might be read - y.

You be - lieve, _____

Yes, she might be read - y.

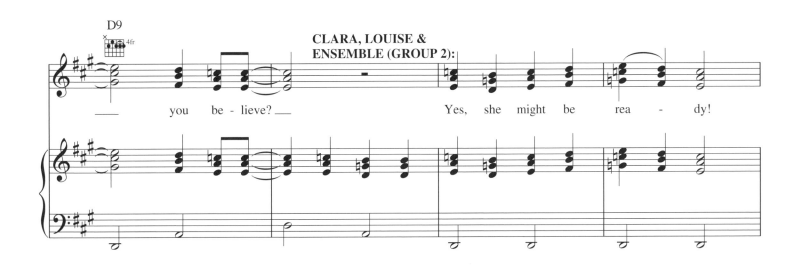

CLARA, LOUISE & ENSEMBLE (GROUP 2):

_____ you be - lieve? _____ Yes, she might be rea - dy!

WITH YOU

Words and Music by GLEN BALLARD,
DAVID ALLAN STEWART and BRUCE JOEL RUBIN

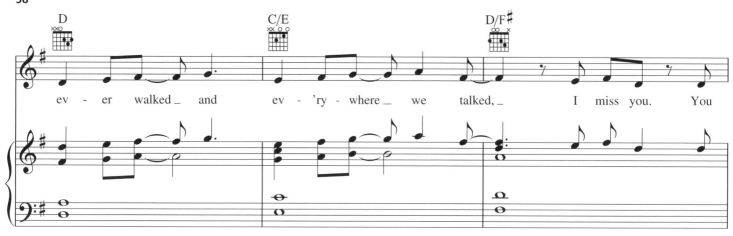

ev - er walked __ and ev - 'ry - where __ we talked, __ I miss you. You

nev - er leave __ my mind. So much __ of you is left __ be - hind. __

Gentle Pop, a little faster

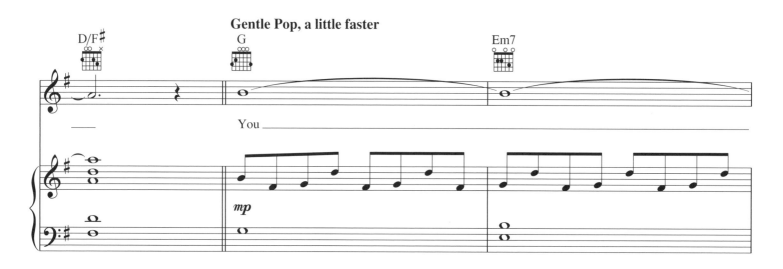

You _____

mp

took __ my days __ with you, _____

SUSPEND MY DISBELIEF/
I HAD A LIFE

Words and Music by GLEN BALLARD,
DAVID ALLAN STEWART and BRUCE JOEL RUBIN

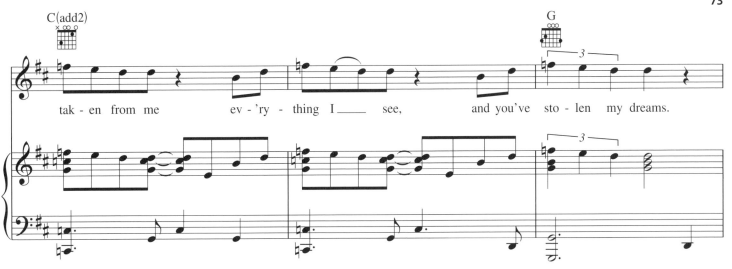

taken from me ev-'ry-thing I ___ see, and you've sto-len my dreams.

MOLLY:

If there's an-y-thing more ___ I can do, ___ I'll

I had a love. ___ This was our ___

do it and find ___ my way back ___ to you. ___ Sus-pend my dis-be-lief. ___

time. You had ___ no right

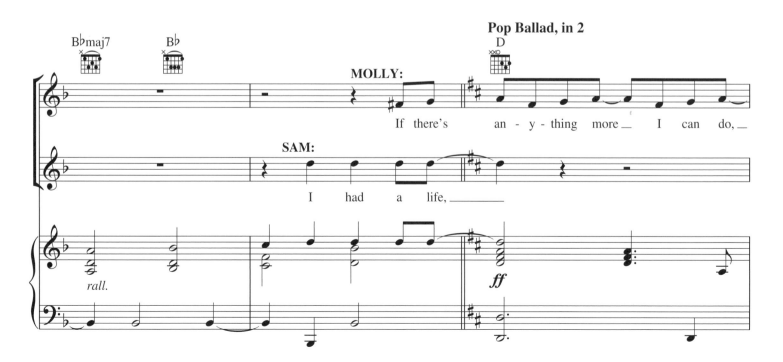

Pop Ballad, in 2

MOLLY: If there's an - y - thing more __ I can do, __

SAM: I had a life, _____

C(add2)

heart. _____

all on ___ loan, __ There's noth-ing you own. __ Noth - ing's for free.

G

now.

Gm

D

Gm/B♭

Here right now. _____

I had a life. ___

This is the life, ___ this is the way ___ we're driv - en.

ENSEMBLE:

This is the life, ___ this is the way ___ we're driv - en.

ff

RAIN/HOLD ON

Words and Music by GLEN BALLARD,
DAVID ALLAN STEWART and BRUCE JOEL RUBIN

I feel you with me now. ___

right   now!

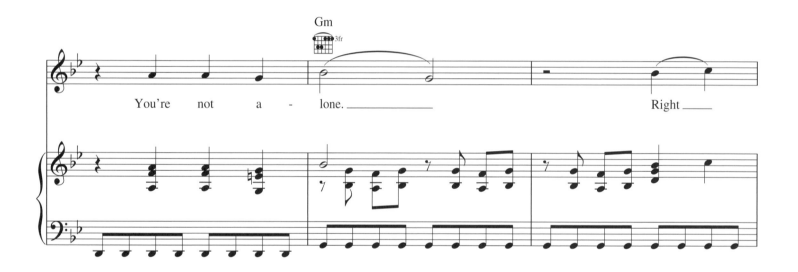

You're not a - lone. _____   Right _____

now,   I want you to know: _____

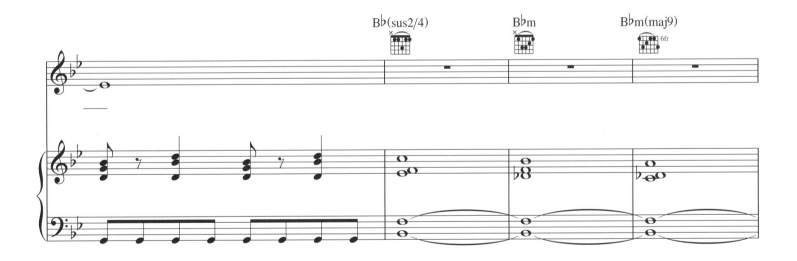

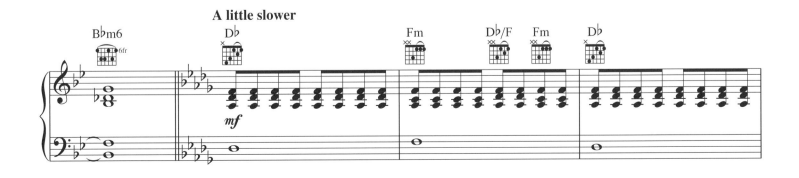

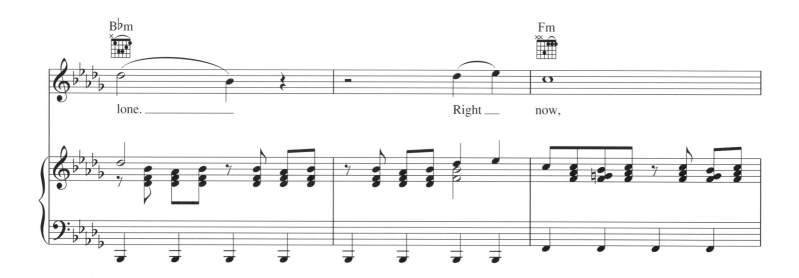

LIFE TURNS ON A DIME

Words and Music by GLEN BALLARD,
DAVID ALLAN STEWART and BRUCE JOEL RUBIN

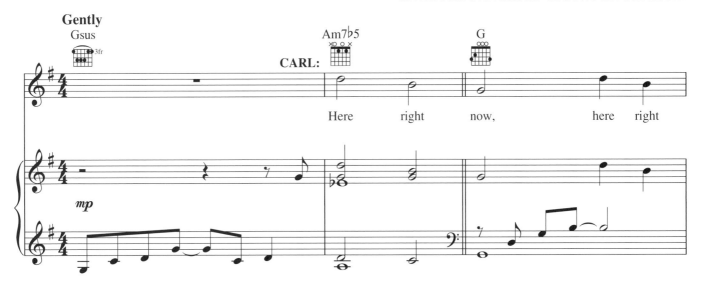

Here right now, here right

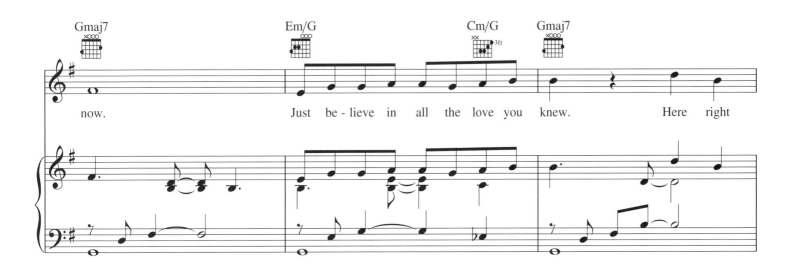

now. Just be-lieve in all the love you knew. Here right

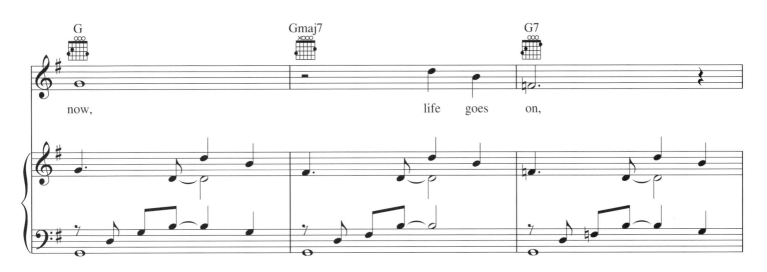

now, life goes on,

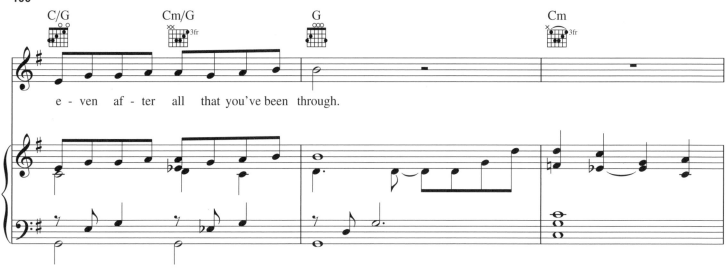

e - ven af - ter all that you've been through.

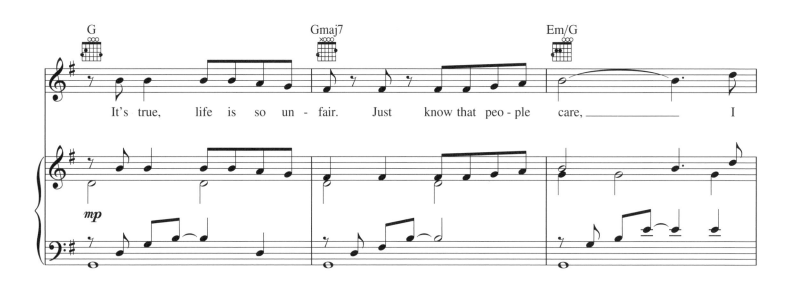

It's true, life is so un - fair. Just know that peo - ple care, _____ I

care. We al - ways think that we'll have time, but then life ___ turns on a

MOLLY: *I think you should leave now.*
CARL: *Molly, you shouldn't be alone.*

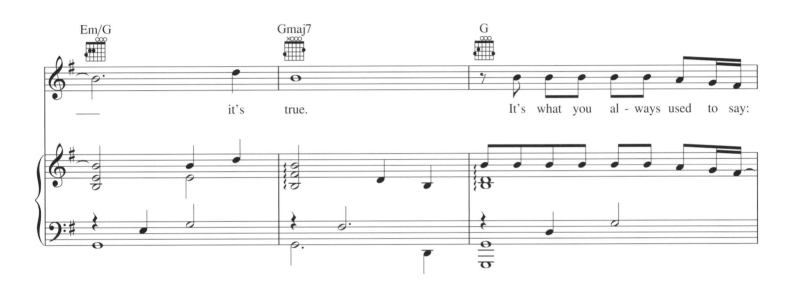

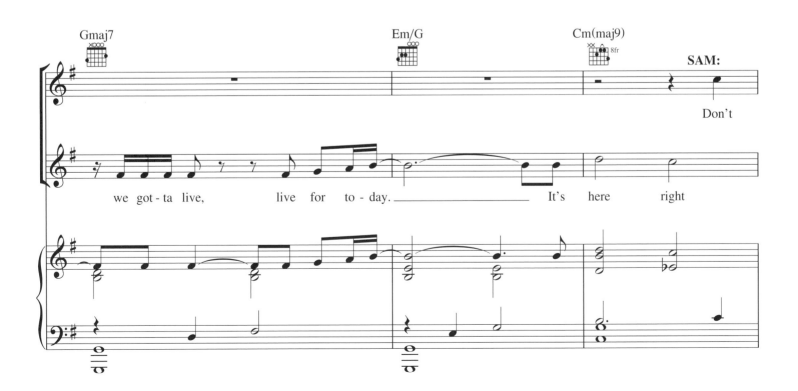

TALKIN' 'BOUT A MIRACLE

Words and Music by GLEN BALLARD,
DAVID ALLAN STEWART and BRUCE JOEL RUBIN

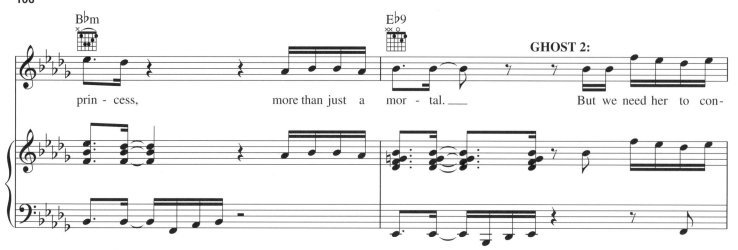

feel him com-in' thru __ now. __

He tells your ma-ma __ hel-lo.

On-ly she can help us all, __ on-ly she can

Db maj7   Csus   C   F

Says Grand-pa

take   us   there.   Yes,   we

Joe's here.

Says he's still a pain in the ass. __

are talk-in' 'bout a mir-a-cle. __

If on-ly she can

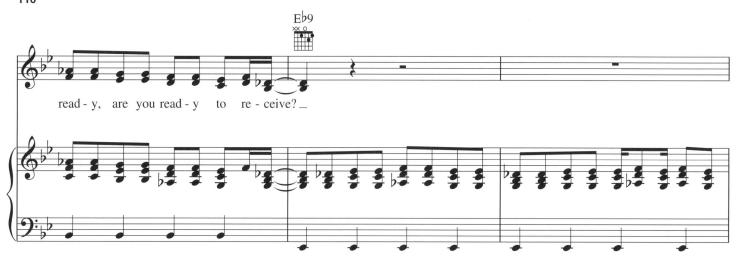

read - y, are you read - y to re - ceive? _

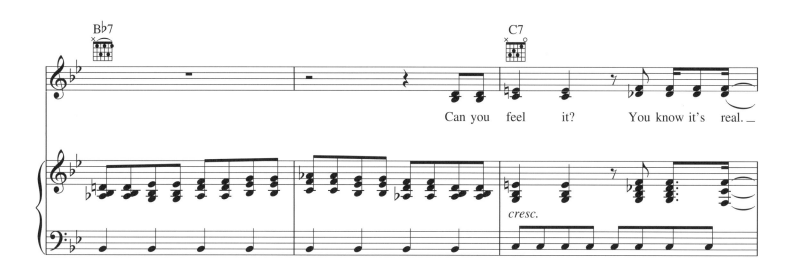

Can you feel it? You know it's real. _

cresc.

Funk (Tempo I)

HOSPITAL GHOST:

She has got the shin - ing, some vi - sion - ar - y

ALL GHOSTS:

Shin - ing,

mf

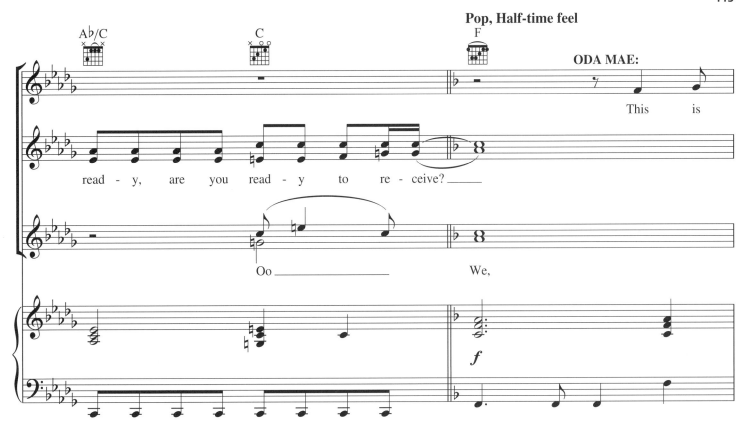

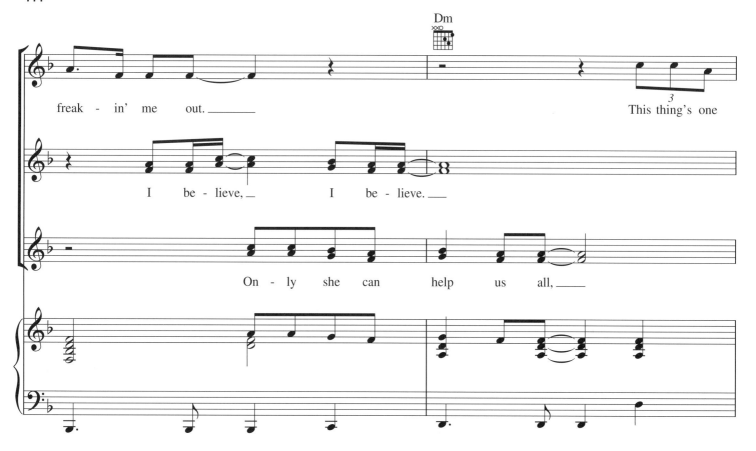

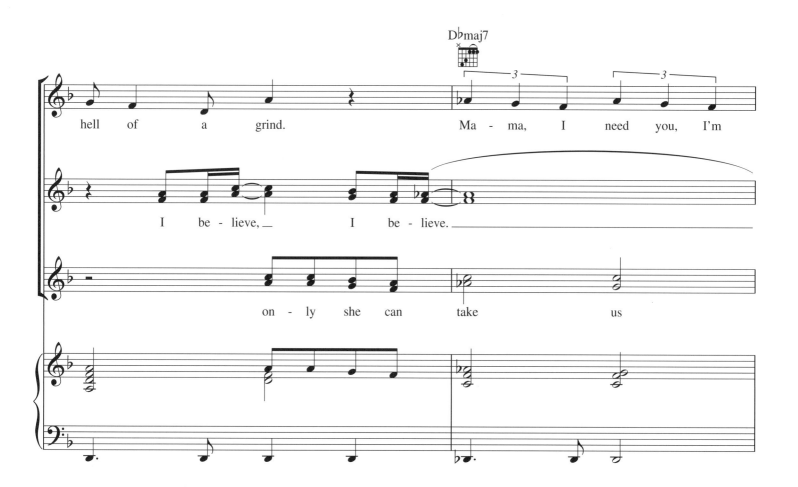

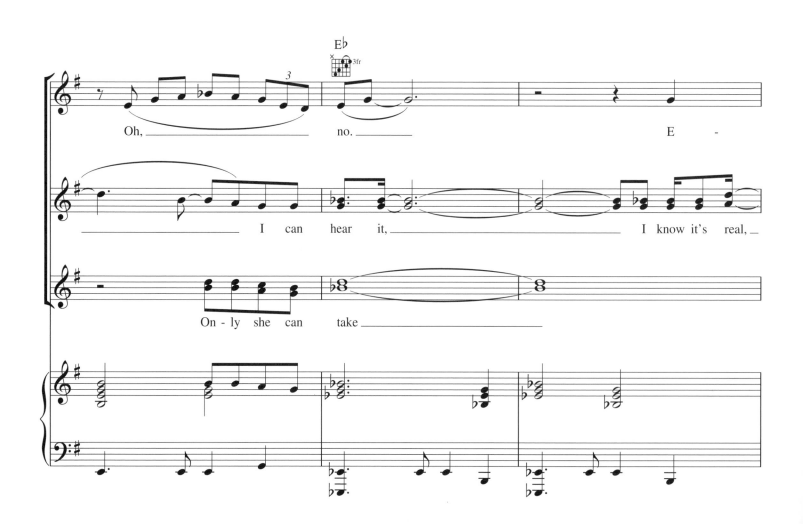

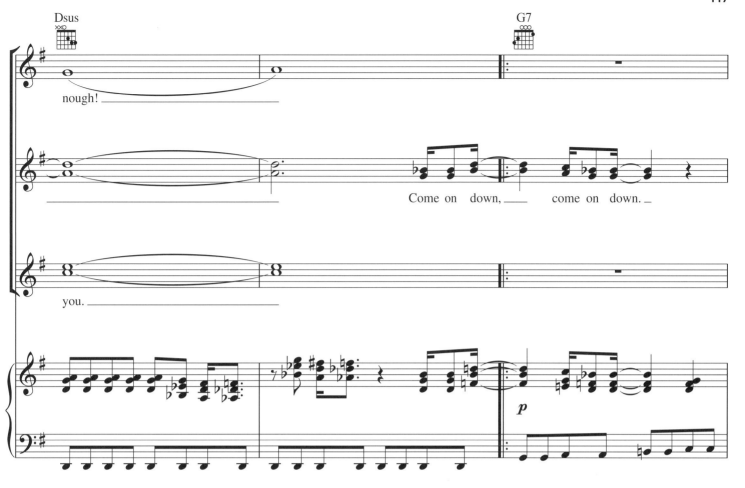

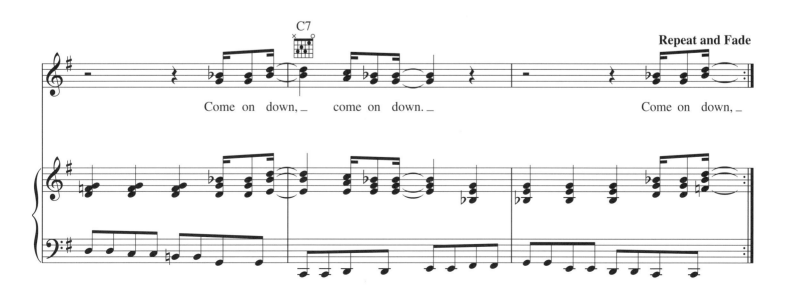

NOTHING STOPS ANOTHER DAY

Words and Music by GLEN BALLARD,
DAVID ALLAN STEWART and BRUCE JOEL RUBIN

Come what may, _____ noth-ing

stops an-oth - er day. _____

- er day. _____
(Vocal 1st time only)

Repeat and Fade

I'M OUTTA HERE

Words and Music by GLEN BALLARD,
DAVID ALLAN STEWART and BRUCE JOEL RUBIN

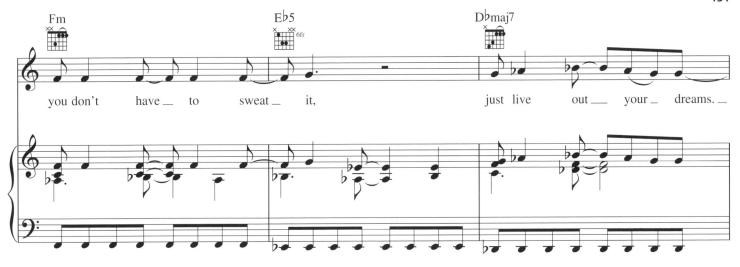